This book was made in collaboration with

Extra learning materials available at www.paulinespreschoolproject.com

More titles in this series:

All about Your Body (about the body)

Copyright © 2023 Clavis Publishing Inc., New York

Originally published as *Kriebels in je buik. Kinderen en seksualiteit. Waar komen baby's vandaan?*
in Belgium and the Netherlands by Clavis Uitgeverij, 2019
English translation from the Dutch by Clavis Publishing Inc., New York

Visit us on the Web at www.clavis-publishing.com.

Butterflies in Your Belly. Where Do Babies Come From? written and illustrated by Pauline Oud

ISBN 978-1-60537-962-3

This book was printed in February 2024 at Nikara, M. R. Štefánika 858/25, 963 01 Krupina, Slovakia.

First Edition
10 9 8 7 6 5 4 3 2

Clavis Publishing supports the First Amendment and celebrates the right to read.

Where Do
Babies Come From?

Pauline Oud

Clavis

NEW YORK

Party

"Cake!" Noa calls out.

Mommy looks very happy.

"We have something to celebrate with you!"

"You're going to have a baby brother or sister,"

Daddy says with a smile.

"The baby is still as small as the strawberry

on your cake," says Mommy.

"But it'll grow and grow, and then

you'll have a baby brother or sister."

Noa takes a little bite from the cake and thinks for a while.

"But how did the baby get there?" she asks.

"Well," says Mommy,

"that's an interesting story."

Eggs and sperm cells

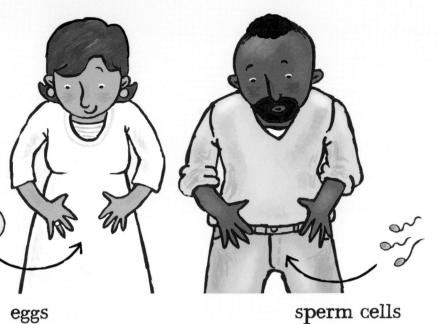

eggs   sperm cells

Eggs and sperm cells grow in the bodies of grown-ups. Eggs grow in a woman's ovaries. Sperm cells grow in a man's testicles. The eggs and sperm cells are so small that you can't see them.

When adults make love or have sex, lots of sperm cells from the man's testicles go up through the woman's vagina and into her body, where they try to find an egg. It's kind of like a treasure hunt!

Only one sperm cell can win

When the winning sperm cell enters the egg, that creates a baby. The baby will grow inside a special place called the woman's uterus, or her womb. It takes a very long time. Because the little egg with the sperm cell in it is still so small, you can hardly see it. It has to grow for nine months to be big enough to be born!

How do the sperm cells get
into Mommy's belly

Operation

"A baby is growing in my mommy's belly,"

Noa tells Luke as they play animal doctor.

"Mommy and Daddy were making love, and then

Daddy put a sperm cell inside the egg in Mommy's belly.

That's why a baby is growing in there now."

Luke has to think about that.

"How did your dad put that sperm cell in your mom's belly?" he asks.

Noa and Luke look at Noa's doctor kit.

"Maybe through her belly button?"

"I think they had to operate," says Luke.

"Yeah," says Noa. "I bet she had an operation on her belly button,

and that's how the baby got in there."

When adults want to **make a baby**,
it often begins with kissing.
It feels good to **kiss** and **hug** each other tight.

Then they might go to their bedroom,
where there's more room and it's **private**.
The mommy and daddy take off their clothes
and cuddle under the covers.

The daddy puts his penis inside the mommy's
vagina. Then fluid with sperm cells travels out
of the daddy's penis into the mommy's vagina
and up into her uterus and ovaries to find an egg.

Small people, big people

It's not only your arms and legs that will grow when you get bigger. Take a look at what else is growing.

Only adults can make babies. Children have to grow first.

If you're a **girl**, you'll become a **woman**.

You'll get breasts, hair will grow near your vagina, and eggs will grow in your ovaries.

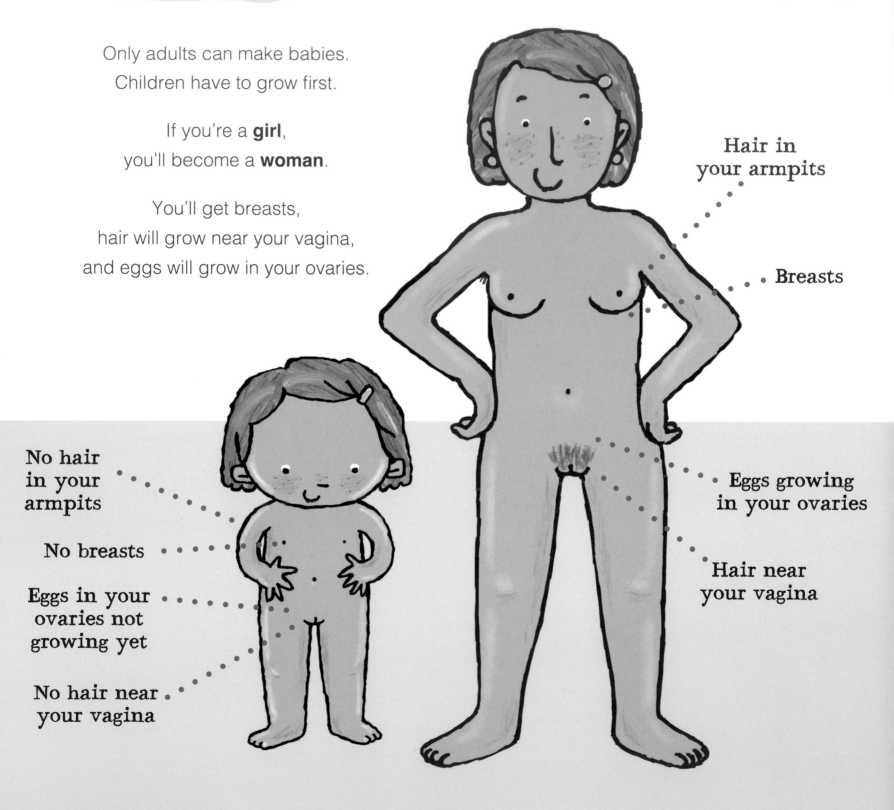

Hair in your armpits

Breasts

Eggs growing in your ovaries

Hair near your vagina

No hair in your armpits

No breasts

Eggs in your ovaries not growing yet

No hair near your vagina

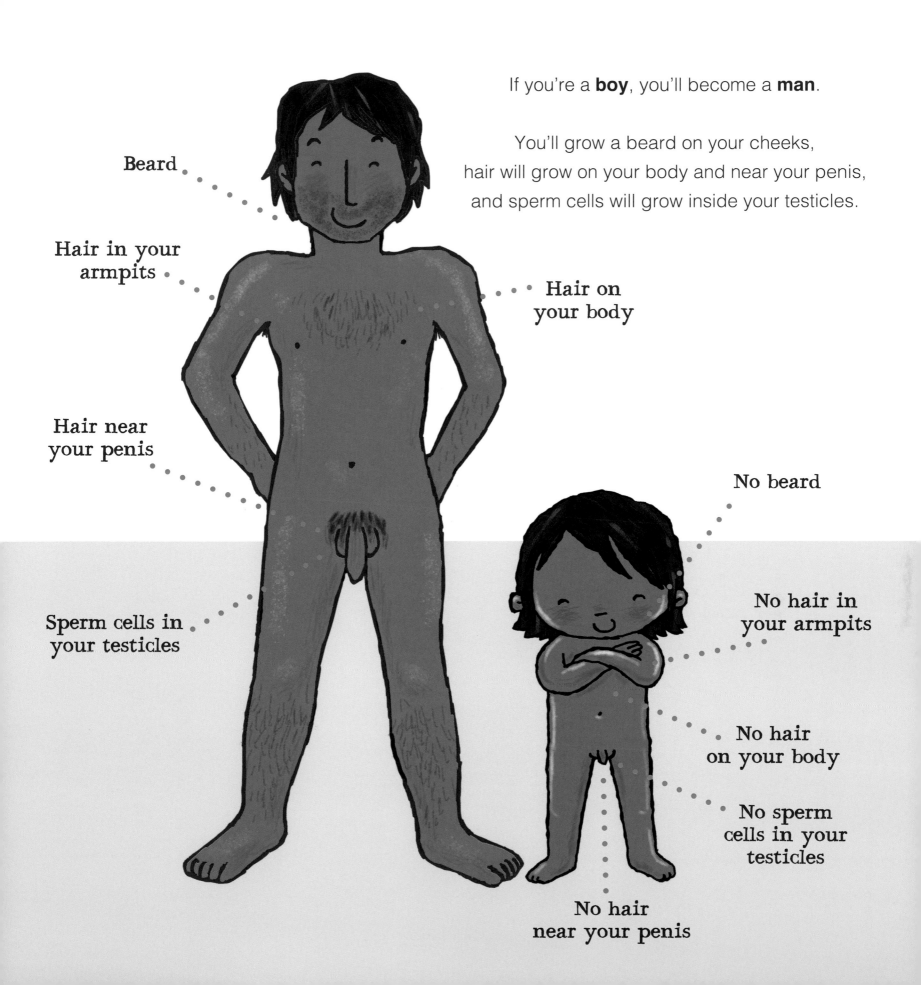

If you're a **boy**, you'll become a **man**.

You'll grow a beard on your cheeks,
hair will grow on your body and near your penis,
and sperm cells will grow inside your testicles.

Beard

Hair in your
armpits

Hair on
your body

Hair near
your penis

No beard

Sperm cells in
your testicles

No hair in
your armpits

No hair
on your body

No sperm
cells in your
testicles

No hair
near your penis

Two mommies

An egg

"Did I start out as an egg too?" Luke asks his mommies.

"And a sperm cell? And a baby?"

"Of course. You grew inside Mommy Lucy's belly."

Luke looks at Mommy Ellen.

"And did you put daddy sperm cells inside Mommy Lucy's belly?"

"No," says Mommy Ellen. "You need a man and a woman to make a baby.

Two women can't make a baby, and two men can't make a baby."

Mommy Lucy looks lovingly at Mommy Ellen.

"But we really wanted a baby together."

The doctor takes the sperm cells out of the little cup and puts them inside the mom's vagina with a syringe. From there, they swim up into her body and try to find an egg.

"So, the doctor put sperm cells inside my body."
Luke gets it now. "I have a Mommy Lucy,
a Mommy Ellen, and the doctor is my dad!"
The mommies laugh. "No, that was not the case.
We don't know who gave the doctor your sperm cells,
but we're very happy someone shared theirs with us."
"I'm sure the sperm cell dad is really nice,"
Luke says with a smile.

Belly

"Is there a baby in your belly?" Liv asks Grandpa.
"Oh, no. I just ate too much. And babies only grow
inside women's bodies. Never in men's bodies.
But when two men want to have a baby together,
they can do that with some help, and sometimes
the babies can have an extra mommy!"
Liv likes that idea. A big family! Then you'll
get lots of presents when it's your birthday!

When two men love each other,
they sometimes want to have a baby together.
A woman can have a baby for them.
Or sometimes they adopt a baby.

"Well, I'd love to have another baby, you know," says Grandma.
"Another sweet, cute little baby.
What do you think, Grandpa?" Grandma smiles.
"Yes, Grandpa! Why don't you have a baby?"
Liv says cheerfully.
"Well, that's not possible," Grandpa says with a sigh.
"To have a baby, you not only have to be a woman,
but you also have to be a lot younger."
"Ah, yes," says Grandma. "That's true.
I'm a bit too old to let a baby grow in my belly."
"That's too bad," says Liv. "I sure would like
a little Grandpa-and-Grandma baby to play with."

Babies only grow in the bellies of younger women. Grandmas have children too, but they're already big!

Swoosh, swoosh, swoosh

Noa's mommy is lying on a tall bed. Her belly is bare.

The doctor touches Mommy's belly with his hands. "The baby grew a lot, and so did your belly," he says. "Put your hands over here, Noa. You can feel the baby kick."

"Oh, yes," Noa says. She feels soft pushes against her hands.

Then the doctor moves a small device over Mommy's belly. "Now, let's be very quiet and listen for the baby," says the doctor. At first, Noa doesn't hear anything. But then . . . *lub-dup, lup-dup* . . . Mommy smiles at Noa. "That's the baby's little heart," she whispers. "We can hear one strong and healthy little heart. From one baby, not two!"

"Two babies? Can that happen?" Noa asks.

"Sure," says the doctor. "Sometimes. Then you're having twins."

"Well, one baby is enough," Mommy laughs.

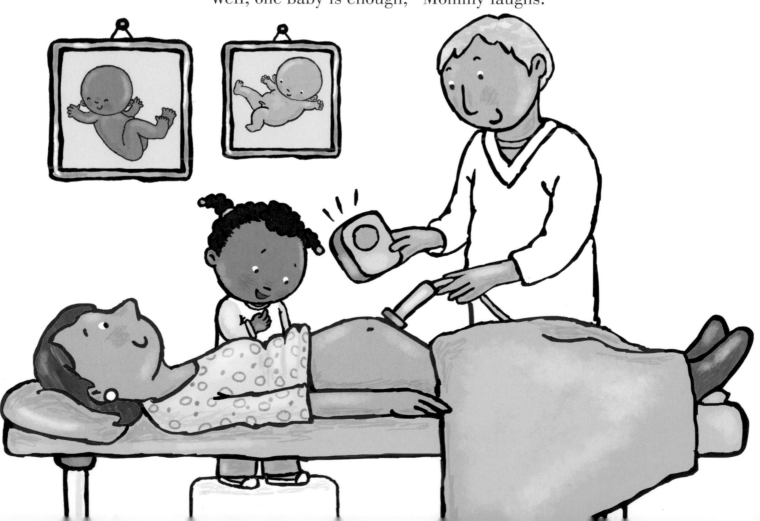

Usually, one baby grows inside the uterus.
But sometimes there are two, and they're called twins.
That can happen when Mommy doesn't have just
one egg but two. Then **two sperm cells** can win.
Two babies will grow in her belly.
One baby can be a boy and the other a girl.
Or they can both be boys or both be girls.

Sometimes, two babies can grow out of **one egg** and
one sperm cell. They're always two girls or two boys.
And they often **look very similar**.

Have you ever seen twins?
Would you like to be a twin?

When a mom is
having twins, her belly is
extra-big. Because the twins
have to share the belly, there
isn't much room to grow.
They're often born a bit early.

How does the baby eat
in Mommy's belly?

Cookies

Noa and Mommy are reading books together and eating cookies.

"Yummy, isn't it?" Noa says.

Mommy's big belly is just like a soft pillow. Every now and then,
Noa feels a little kick. Then the baby moves inside Mommy's belly.

"How many cookies did you have?" Mommy asks.

"Only one," says Noa. She takes a big bite
from her third cookie. Mmm, that tastes good.

"I think the baby wants to have another cookie too," says Noa.

"You have to eat it. Then the cookie can make its way to the baby."

"Well, then give me another one," Mommy says, smiling.

Noa takes a cookie from the tin. It's for the baby.

Now there's only one cookie left. Gulp!

And now that one's gone too.

It's inside Noa's belly.

The baby is lying in a big bag of water in Mommy's uterus. There's a **tube** attached to the baby's belly and to Mommy's uterus. It's called the **umbilical cord**. The baby **eats** and **breathes** and gets everything it needs to grow through the umbilical cord. It gets a bit of everything Mommy eats. When the baby is born, it can eat and breathe on its own. Then it doesn't need the umbilical cord anymore.

The baby is growing. Mommy's belly is growing too. Her uterus is getting bigger and bigger. When the baby is still small, there's a lot of space. When the baby grows, it only just fits. Then you can feel the baby move.

Take a look at your belly. Can you find your belly button? Everyone has one. Because that's where you were attached to your mommy in her belly.

Airplane

"Let's take a walk with baby bear," says Mika.

"Yes!" Rafi says. "Baby bear, do you hear that airplane way up high?

My mommy and daddy came to get me in an airplane.

I was born in a different city. My belly mommy

and my sperm cell daddy couldn't take care of me.

And Daddy and Mommy could!"

"I'm so happy they brought you here," smiles Mika.

"Me too! And this is our baby, right?" asks Rafi.

"I'm the daddy, and you're the mommy."

"Yes," says Mika. "And we adopted our baby too!"

All children grew from an egg of a mommy
and a sperm cell of a daddy.
That's why some people look a little like
their daddy, mommy, brothers, and sisters.

Liv and her daddy both have red hair.

Noa's daddy has dark brown skin,
and her mother has light skin. Noa's skin is tan.

Luke's mommy wears glasses.
Luke can't see very well without his glasses either.

Adoption

Sometimes a mommy and daddy can't take care of
their baby. When they're very ill, for instance, or maybe
they have died. And there are also mommies and daddies
who want a baby but maybe their bodies won't let them.
Then the new mommy and daddy adopt the child.

Rafi didn't come from the egg and
the sperm cell of his mommy
and daddy. That's why he
doesn't look like his mommy
and daddy.

Baby bath

"Open it," says Mommy.

Noa is helping out.

Together, they're looking through all the boxes.

"Look," says Noa. "Doll clothes!"

"No," laughs Mommy. "Those are baby clothes!

And not just any baby clothes. Those were *your* baby clothes."

Noa can't believe it.

"Oh, yes," says Mommy. "That's how small you were.

And when the baby is born,

he or she will fit in your baby clothes."

"Look! There's the crib," Noa says.

"We'll need that too. And the baby bath."

Noa puts the bath on the ground. She still fits perfectly!

Even though babies are very small,
they need a lot of things.

A baby bath

A playpen

A crib

Diapers

Baby clothes

Toys

A stroller

A pacifier

Bottles

A new room for the baby

"Look! This is the bedroom for the baby," says Noa.
"It was my room first, but I got too big for such a little room."
Noa and Tom ride the horse into the baby's bedroom.
"What's that?" asks Tom.
He pushes his finger into the changing mat.
"That's what the baby has to lie on
when it gets a new diaper."

"And what's that?"
"That's a crib. It's a bed for babies."
"Why is there a tent around it?"
"Babies think that's cozy," says Noa.
"No playing in the baby's bedroom!" Daddy calls from downstairs.
"We aren't!" Noa and Tom quickly ride the horse into the room next door.
"We're playing in my new bedroom!"

"I got to pick the paint color all by myself."

"Paint?" asks Tom.

"On the wall," says Noa as she points.

"I wanted blue at first, but now orange is my favorite color.

And my bed is new too. Big, right?" Noa jumps on her bed.

Tom takes the horse and puts it on Noa's new bed.

"Look," says Tom. "We can make a tent bed too."

They pull the comforter over the horse. It's very cozy.

"Daddy!" Noa calls downstairs. "Can Tom spend the night?

We made a crib for big kids!"

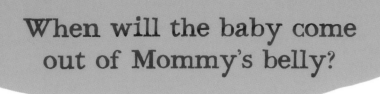

When will the baby come
out of Mommy's belly?

Birthday

"Don't run so fast," Mommy says, panting.

"My belly is too big to go any faster."

But Noa can hardly wait. Today is her birthday.

She gets to hand out treats to everyone in class.

"Happy birthday, birthday girl," Mr. John says with a smile.

"When will the baby be born?"

"Soon," says Noa. "Because today is my birthday,

and then we're going on vacation, and then the baby will be here."

"Yes," Mommy says. "And I'm sure the baby will

want to get out of my belly after our vacation."

"The baby has to grow first until it's ready.

And then it comes out through the vagina!" Noa explains.

"Well, well," says Mr. John. "You know exactly how it works!

Come inside, and then we'll sing for you, birthday big sister."

"I'm not a big sister yet!" Noa laughs.

"Not until the baby is born!"

How will the baby come out of Mommy's belly?

Most of the time no one knows exactly **when** the baby will come.
Not even the doctor. But the doctor can often predict
how soon it'll be. Some babies come out a little early.
Other babies stay a little longer in their mommy's belly.

When the baby wants to come out, Mommy feels it in her belly.
Very slowly, the muscles in her uterus push the baby down toward
her vagina. Sometimes, it takes an entire day or night.
Mommy's vagina slowly gets wider.
Wide enough for the baby's head to fit through.
First the head comes out. Then the little body and
finally the little legs. The baby is still attached to Mommy with
the umbilical cord. The cord isn't needed anymore and is cut.
That doesn't hurt. The baby can breathe on its own and drink from
Mommy or a bottle. The baby can finally get hugs and kisses!

Too soon

Sometimes, a baby is born too soon.
Then it has to stay in the hospital for a while.
The baby stays in a special warm bed
called an incubator. That way, the doctor
can keep an eye on everything until
the baby is ready to go home.

Will the baby be
a boy or a girl?

Brister

"Daddy," says Noa, "do you know what the baby in Mommy's belly is called?"

"Well," says Daddy, "Mommy and I are still thinking about that.

Because it has to be a very pretty name, of course.

And the prettiest name is already taken. Because that's Noa. And that's your name."

"You should call the baby Mirabellia," says Noa. "Or Sanandia. Or Little Princess."

Daddy thinks about it. "But those are all names for girls.

Maybe you'll get a baby brother."

"Mitchell! Or Rover, just like Luke's dog!" says Noa.

"That's a boy too. I want a brother. Just like Liv. Or no, a sister."

"But when we get back from vacation, you have to know the name," says Noa.

"Because then the baby will be born!"

"Let's call the baby Brister for now," says Daddy.

"Brister?" Noa asks.

"Yes," says Daddy. "Brother-sister, Brister."

"Mommy!" Noa calls. "Our baby is called Brister!"

With a special camera, the doctor makes an **ultrasound image**.
That's a video or **photo of the baby** in Mommy's belly.
Then you can see if it's a boy or a girl.
Many mommies and daddies want to know
if their baby will be a boy or a girl.
Sometimes, they tell everyone.
Or they keep it as a fun little secret.
Other daddies and mommies don't want to know yet.
Then the doctor keeps the secret.
Only after the baby is born will everyone find out.

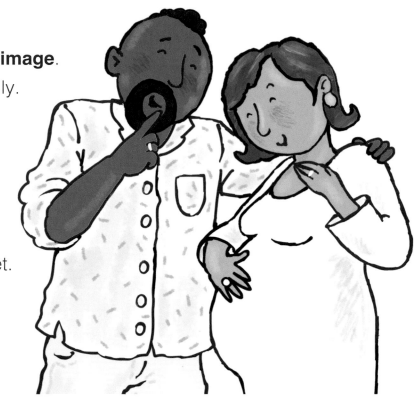

*How can you
tell if the baby
is a boy?
Or a girl?*

All people have their **own name**.
Their daddy and mommy came up with that name.
You got a name **from your parents** too.
They chose your name because they thought
it was a great name for you.
The **name** for the **new baby** is sometimes a **secret**.
Only when the baby is born will everyone
find out the baby's name.

*What's your
favorite name?*

A baby brother!

"Grab your coat and your shoes, Noa,"
Grandma calls. "Then we'll quickly jump in the car.
And don't forget the beautiful drawing you made for the baby!"
"Hooray! The baby has finally arrived!" Noa cheers.
"Shh, not too loud," Daddy whispers when they arrive at the hospital.
Together, they climb the stairs. Mommy is in bed.
At first, Noa doesn't see anything different.
But then she notices Mommy is holding a very tiny baby.
"Look," says Mommy. "This is your baby brother."
"Let's sit down next to Mommy," says Daddy.
"Then you can hold your little brother."
Noa would love that! She holds the baby tight.
"His name is Finn," Daddy says proudly.
"Finn," Noa whispers.
She thinks it's the best name.

Helping the baby

Little babies can't take a bath by themselves.
Or go to the bathroom. Noa gets to help. Together, she and Daddy
give the baby a bath, and they put on a clean diaper too.

Babies have to sleep a lot.
At night and during the day.
Sometimes they cry. If they're in pain,
or if they're hungry, they can't use their words
yet like big kids can. Sometimes they just want
to cuddle. And then they stop crying.

A party for the baby!
Everyone comes to admire the new baby.
There are presents for Noa and for the baby.

Spot the 7 differences!

Is it for Noa?

Who is it for? Go ahead and point!

The shoes

The jeans

The scissors

The shower

The diaper

The overalls

The colored pencils

The shirt

The toy box

The onesie

The blocks

The mobile

The rattle

The cake

The car

The chair

The food

The socks

The crane

The balloon

The jumpsuit

The underpants

The ring tower

The socks

The kite

The stroller

The rattle

The books

The bottle

The cup

The baby bath

The jacket

The toilet

Look! This is how a baby grows

1 month pregnant
The baby is now as big as a grain of rice.

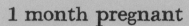

2 months pregnant
The baby is now as big as a grape.

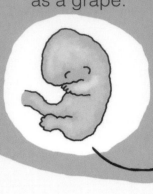
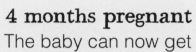

3 months pregnant
The baby is now as big as an orange.

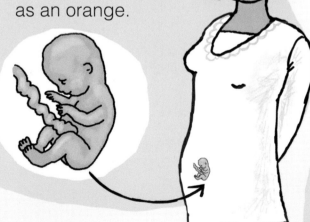
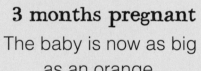

4 months pregnant
The baby can now get the hiccups.

5 months pregnant
The baby can now hear.

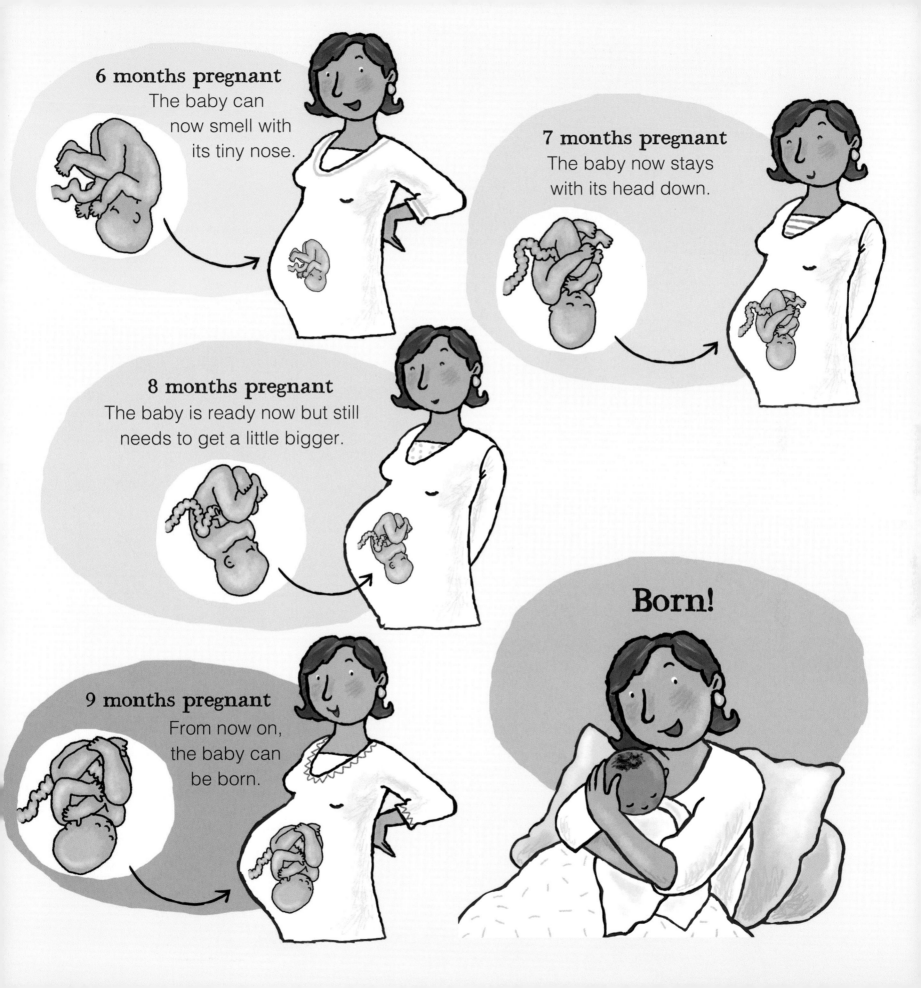

6 months pregnant
The baby can now smell with its tiny nose.

7 months pregnant
The baby now stays with its head down.

8 months pregnant
The baby is ready now but still needs to get a little bigger.

9 months pregnant
From now on, the baby can be born.

Born!